How to Live the Van Life Dream

A Guide to Maximizing Van Life: Camping, Comfort, Cooking, Exercise, Passive Income, Off-Grid Living, Tech, Van Essentials, and More in the USA

Jake Rader, CPA

© **Copyright 2022 - All rights reserved.**

The content contained within this book may not be reproduced, duplicated or transmitted without direct written permission from the author or the publisher.

Under no circumstances will any blame or legal responsibility be held against the publisher, or author, for any damages, reparation, or monetary loss due to the information contained within this book, either directly or indirectly.

Legal Notice:

This book is copyright protected. It is only for personal use. You cannot amend, distribute, sell, use, quote or paraphrase any part, or the content within this book, without the consent of the author or publisher.

Disclaimer Notice:

Please note the information contained within this document is for educational and entertainment purposes only. All effort has been executed to present accurate, up to date, reliable, complete information. No warranties of any kind are declared or implied. Readers acknowledge that the author is not engaged in the rendering of legal, financial, medical or professional advice. The content within this book has been derived from various sources. Please consult a licensed professional before attempting any techniques outlined in this book.

By reading this document, the reader agrees that under no circumstances is the author responsible for any losses, direct or indirect, that are incurred as a result of the use of the information contained within this document, including, but not limited to, errors, omissions, or inaccuracies.

Sign Up Bonus

Just scan the QR code to be the first to know when I launch another book on travel, real estate, or passive income!

As a special bonus, you'll receive:

Top 10 Passive Income Ideas for Building Wealth in 2023
13 Essentials You Need To Know About Before Buying Your First RV

absolutely FREE!

Contents

Introduction	vii
1. BUILDING YOUR DREAM VAN	1
Electrical	3
Insulation	5
Plumbing	7
Layout Mistakes to Avoid	8
2. BUYING A PRE-CONSTRUCTED VAN	11
Where to Buy	11
Non-negotiable Elements for the Best Deals	12
Making Updates	13
3. FINANCING LIFE ON THE ROAD	14
Your Budget	14
Passive Income Tips and Opportunities	16
4. THE BIG BATHROOM QUESTIONS	24
Bathroom Options	24
5. INTERNET AND OTHER TECHNOLOGY	27
Getting Internet on the Road	27
The Best Apps	30
6. GO TO SLEEP WITHOUT COUNTING SHEEP	34
Urban Camping	36
Rural Camping	36
7. VAN LIFE HACKS AND TIPS YOU DIDN'T CONSIDER	39
Laundry	39
Staying Active	41
Cooking	43
Pets	47
8. VAN MAINTENANCE	50
Tools and Essentials You Need to Stay Moving	54

Conclusion 57
Bibliography 67

Introduction

Van life is an exciting and increasingly popular lifestyle for people who reject the typical societal structure of renting an apartment, going to work from nine to five, and saving up to buy a house. It isn't only popular among young people; retirees who want to see the country rather than be tied down to a mortgage have sold their homes and now live full-time in an RV. We are in the midst of a van life boom. Roughly 140,000 people lived out of vans, RVs, or school buses by choice in 2019, and that number has certainly grown in the last few years. Remembering that van life, in the specific way we'll be discussing throughout this book, is a choice rather than an economic necessity—the way some people experiencing homelessness are forced to live in cars or vans—is essential.

You can transition to van life as a solo traveler or a couple. You can bring your dog, or any other pet, on the road too! There are even some families who have committed themselves to travel full-time. Whatever your current lifestyle, it can be adapted to van life.

If you are considering downsizing your life in favor of adventure and nomadism, then you've come to the right place.

I am just like you, a van lifer who wants to help others achieve their dreams of living in a van and seeing all this beautiful country has to offer. I'm a CPA and real estate investor who lately has dedicated himself

Introduction

to traveling full-time. I've traveled from Seattle to Key West and back again, and now I want to share my knowledge with prospective van lifers. Taking the plunge into van life may seem intimidating, but I want to remove that fear barrier by handing you the tools and knowledge you need to buy a van, get on the road, and embrace traveling full-time.

Throughout this book, we are going to cover the basics of converting your van, how to buy a pre-built model, and how to earn passive income on the road. Passive income is one of my particular areas of expertise, so pay close attention to Chapter 3 if you are looking to reinvent the way you earn money. We will also explore common questions like where to go to the bathroom and sleep, how to get internet, and even some of the questions you may not have considered yet—like how to do laundry, what are the best cooking methods, and what are the most helpful apps for making life on the road easier.

I'll also share some of the best road trips and destinations around the country, so if you need inspiration for where to drive first, I'll help you make those decisions too. Van life doesn't have to be an isolating experience; it can be filled with community and helpful advice.

You should put your key in the ignition with confidence in the quality of your conversion, the game plan for making money, and all the day-to-day activities that change when you no longer have a permanent home base. Embrace the once-in-a-lifetime experience of doing something truly new, take in jaw-dropping scenery, and see how van life can change your perspectives and priorities. There is no one way to live life, and by exploring van life, you are taking the first step towards grabbing the reins of life and setting a new course.

Chapter 1
Building Your Dream Van

One of the most popular options for van lifers is to build out their own van. When you build the van yourself, all the decisions are up to you—the layout, the electricity, the plumbing, and even what kind of van you start with. The best part of building your dream van is that you don't need extensive woodworking experience to create a van interior that will work for you.

Sprinter vans, or comparable models, are the most common style of a van used for full-time van life. They are produced by Mercedes Benz, Ford, Dodge, and others. If you have your eye on a brand new model, the base price for the Mercedes Benz Sprinter Van is currently $38,000. Because of that high sticker price, most van lifers opt for purchasing used vans. Websites like Facebook Marketplace, Auto Trader, and Craigslist are great places to start looking for vans that have not already been converted into living spaces. Used Sprinter vans typically start at $3,000 and can go up to $20,000 depending on how old they are, how many miles are on the van, and how recently features like brakes have been updated.

You may find a van for under $5,000, but remember the older a vehicle is, the more likely it will need repairs in the next few years. If the van breaks down, fixing it isn't something that can be put off. That is your home. It needs to be in tip-top shape.

Jake Rader, CPA

Deciding which car manufacturer's van to purchase is a big decision. Don't let price be the only consideration. Evaluate the size, fuel economy, and repair costs of the van. Below are some of the notable perks for each of the different makes and models of vans currently available.

Mercedez Benz Sprinter Van

- Factory standard 4x4 options
- 20 miles per gallon
- Available in diesel options
- Standard 400,000 miles over the life of the vehicle
- Tall enough for most people to stand up inside

Ford Transit Van

- All-wheel drive option
- Less expensive purchase price
- Low maintenance costs and easy to find parts
- Tallest interior height of any van on the market

Dodge Promaster Van

- Easiest van to convert for living full-time due to interior wall shape
- Front-wheel drive
- 18 miles per gallon
- Shortest of all the available vans on the market

Based on these basic outlines, you may already have an idea of which van will best fit your lifestyle. For those who envision traveling off-grid and up the mountains more often, then the four-wheel drive and all-wheel drive options may be best. For van lifers who are looking to build their dream van with the most customizations, then the Dodge van may be the best option. There are other less popular van options, like the Chevy Express or the GMC Savana, that can still work well for van life but have some unique features that require extra research.

How to Live the Van Life Dream

Once you have a van parked in the driveway, ready to be built out, make sure you have some basic tools handy before diving into the project.

Some of the tools are basic and obvious like a tape measure and a utility knife. Others, like a drill and a jigsaw, are a bit more niche. Make sure to factor in purchasing tools to your budget if you don't already have these at home. Most hardware stores have a rental service, so if you don't want to commit to owning a jigsaw, it could be rentable by the weekend. You'll also want a level or straight edge, extra drill bits, and of course, wood.

The wood will create the frame for your bed and the storage around the van. Features like cabinets or shelves can be purchased whole, or you could become your own Bob the Builder and create these items yourself. It all depends on your comfort level.

Electrical

Electricity is the most important element of a van build because so many of the tools we rely on every day need electricity to charge and function. The first decision you'll have to make is what kind of power source you want to rely on. Solar is very popular among van lifers, but you can also use power stations or the van's USB or voltage chargers for small electronics. A mixture of all of these options works well too!

If you don't have any prior experience working with electricity, then be sure to consult a professional for exact advice for your specific situation.

Let's focus on solar first. If there are solar panels on your van, then the sun charges the solar panels which transfer that energy to a charge controller. The charge controller then transmits that power to the lights and batteries in the van. Your electronics can be connected to the batteries via an inverter. As long as it is bright and sunny outside, you'll be able to rely on solar power. That inverter is essential for any three-pronged electronics like computers.

Before purchasing or installing solar power, you'll need to know how much electricity you use on a daily basis. Until you are moving into a van, it is likely that you've never considered the exact amount of electricity that you use. This information will help you save space and money. Start by listing out all of your items that rely on electricity, like lights and computers. Then look up the watts each of those items draw. You can likely find that information on the packaging or by a quick internet search. Next, consider how many hours of each day you will be using each product. Just get within the ballpark. There will obviously be some days that you work on the computer more than others.

Multiply the total watts across all your products by the total number of hours each one will be used. That watt-hours number is how much electricity you'll use in a day. A desktop computer typically requires 65 to 200 watts, so let's average that out around 100 watts. If you are using your computer for three hours per day, then the watts-hour for the computer is 300.

Now that you know how many watt-hours your products need on any given day, you'll need to know what size battery to get for your space. To determine battery size, you'll need to calculate amp-hours or watt-hours divided by battery voltage. Let's say you have a 12-volt battery and the van's total watt-hours are 1,000. Divide 1,000 watt-hours by 12 volts and you'll need a battery that runs at least 83.3 amp-hours. Always purchase a battery that is capable of more amp-hours than you calculate that you'll need. This will increase the battery's life span.

Finally, choose the right solar panel. Solar panels are sold by watts. Remember your original watts-hour number? You'll need that number again! Estimate the total hours of sunlight your solar panels will see each day. Ideally, that is between six and eight hours, being conservative, but that number will fluctuate depending on the season and where you are in the country. Divide your watts-hour number by the total number of daylight hours. The resulting number is how many watts of solar panel you will need.

For example, if you have 1,000 watt-hours divided by six hours of daylight, you would require a 167-watt solar panel. Always round up, because you will have overcast days and days of higher energy consumption.

Non-solar options, like a power station, will require much less math and they are less expensive. They are also less reliable than solar power. If you are only living in the van part-time, then the power stations are a fantastic option. They can easily charge a mini fridge, a few laptop charges, fans, or the lighting in the van, but they cannot continue to do so for as long as solar.

Popular models on the market include Goal Zero and Renogy. These have multiple ports for plugging in your cords. They are also easy to transport in and out of the van.

Insulation

Without insulation, the van is going to get cold at night. Keeping the keys in the ignition to run heat or air conditioning in the summer is not a realistic option. You'll burn out the battery and waste gas. Insulation can also keep out noises, so you'll sleep soundly all night.

The proper van insulation is a balance between price, space, and R-value. R-value is a rating of how effectively insulation keeps heat from leaving or entering your space. Insulation with a higher R-value is thicker. Unfortunately, the thicker the insulation you install, the less space you'll have in the van in all directions. Insulation in a van doesn't stop at the walls. You'll be insulating the floors and the ceiling as well, and then covering with wood, metal, or another material.

Before you start insulating the van, make sure that any materials going behind the walls have already been installed. This can include wiring or plumbing. Imagine breaking through the insulation to hide wires and pipes! Don't go out of order here.

Begin with the floor. Not everyone insulates the floor of the van because heat rises. Thankfully, if you do choose to insulate the floor, you can use a lower R-value insulation or just plywood before covering the floor with whatever material you choose for the true floor of the van.

For the easiest installation, use cardboard to trace any difficult corners or inconsistencies around the floor. Lay the cardboard over your chosen insulation and cut to shape. The insulation can be laid down and secured with Gorilla Tape or something similar.

Insulating the wheel wells is the next step. If you are using spray foam insulation for the walls, then you can cover the wheel wells with this insulation as well. If you aren't using spray foam insulation on the walls, you can always opt for aluminum rolls or bubble-foil materials. Fatmat Rattletrap is a soundproofing material that also works well on wheel wells while reducing road noise.

Once the floor and wheels are covered, you can move on to the walls. If your van of choice has a rigid, box-like structure, then stiff insulation without much flexibility will work well, like foam panels. If your van has a cylindrical structure, then you'll want to invest in a more flexible material, like spray foam. Attaching the rigid panels is easy. Most of the time they can be pressed into place. The foam insulation is more expensive and time-consuming to install. You'll need the spray cans sold at most hardware stores, but any uneven areas on the walls will be difficult to cover up later. Be prepared; it is extremely difficult to remove spray foam insulation, so you won't get more than one shot. With a little patience and money, it can be the best option, no matter the shape of the van.

You can insulate the ceiling of the van with the same material you used for the walls. The thickest portion of insulation should be on the ceiling, because of the nature of heat to rise. Try to install one to two inches of insulation on the ceiling for best results. Once again, make sure that all wiring, lighting, and plumbing have already been placed on the ceiling before you place the insulation.

The windows are the last key insulation point in the van. They reflect a large amount of heat into the van in the summer months, so using a reflective surface that can rebound the sun's rays out of the van will be essential to keeping cool. Curtains and windshield covers are easy-to-find products that also help the heat that is gained and lost through windows. Ensure that the windows are thoroughly sealed and take the time to plug any holes at this point.

Plumbing

Plumbing is a 'nice-to-have' not a 'need-to-have' feature in a van conversion. In Chapter 4, we will take an in-depth look at the big bathroom questions most people have about living in a van. For now, we will examine the details you'll need to have if you do plan on installing plumbing in the van. Running water can transform your van from a weekend getaway to a full-time possibility, but this step of the build will take time and money.

First, you'll need to choose a water tank. Water tanks allow you to have fresh water for drinking and cooking. These tanks have exterior models that are larger, holding up to 45 gallons at a time, and interior models that are smaller. Interior water tanks are easier to refill at water stations than the exterior models, but you'll need to find a layout that leaves room for the tank inside the van.

A gray water system or a process for handling the used, dirty water should also be on your shopping list. Some people prefer to cut a hole in the bottom of the van floor. The sink pipes would flow directly into this hole for easy water disposal. You could also install interior or exterior gray water tanks. These work opposite to the water tank discussed above. Rather than holding fresh water, they hold the dirty water and you can dump them whenever is convenient. The interior gray water tank is the most popular option among van lifers because it is easy to empty whenever you stop without having to disconnect several pipes and brackets like you do with the exterior tank. Once again, just ensure you've considered the space this tank will use when designing the layout of the van.

A pump will allow you to have real, running water from these tanks. There are two varieties of pumps for van lifers to choose from: manual and electric. The manual models are less expensive, conserve more water, and are easy to install. A pedal for your foot or hand is installed next to the sink and water is pushed out with each pump of the pedal. Keep in mind that water filters cannot be installed on manual options. The electric system, meanwhile, can include a water filter. These 12-volt pumps get their power from your solar power system or power station. The water from an electric pump is much more pressurized than the water from a manual pump, but these options are more expensive and harder to install. They also use more water than the manual pump.

Consult a professional before diving into the intricacies of plumbing your van. The general to-do list you will follow includes mounting the pump, attaching the pipes from the tank to your sink and faucet, connecting the hot and cold water lines, connecting the filter (if you are using one), and connecting the gray tank to the pipe system. Remember to use plumbing tape on all of your connections. The last thing you want is water in the van.

Layout Mistakes to Avoid

When creating a layout for the van, you need to consider your specific lifestyle. Are you living in the van full-time? Part-time? Only taking it out for weekend trips or vacations? This will seriously impact how many amenities you want to include.

If you are traveling alone, then you'll have more space. But, even one extra person or one extra dog creates a whole new set of layout considerations.

There are three main zones in most van layouts: the kitchen, the bed, and the hangout or workspace. Where you place all of these will depend on your answers to the previous questions. The biggest consideration that most people miss is comparing your height to the width of the van. In many layouts, the bed is placed at the back of the van so that you sleep horizontally across the van, but if you are more than six feet tall, you might not sleep comfortably in that position. Exceptionally tall van lifers should layout their van so the bed is longer and more narrow; perhaps it could convert into a sitting area along the side of the van.

A few common layouts include:

- placing the bed horizontally at the back, the kitchen along one wall, and a desk or additional seating on the opposite wall

- placing the bed lengthwise along a wall, with the kitchen in the far back, and additional seating across from the bed
- or, placing a bed directly behind the driver's seat, the kitchen along the wall, and additional seating in the back

Never forgo that additional seating or workspace. Assuming that you can sit on your bed or the driver's seat all the time is not realistic. If you are working remotely or running a passive income gig from the van, you'll want that working space. And, if you are traveling with a partner, you'll want the space to spread out and not constantly sit next to one another.

Some vans will have a high enough ceiling for you to loft your sleeping space. With the bed removed from the ground, you could use the underside for storage or another seating area. Be sure to consult a construction or woodworking professional when lofting the bed. The structure needs to be stable enough to hold your weight! Even lifting your bed a few feet off the ground can be great for extra storage, in case you don't want to sleep five or more feet above the floor.

Minimalism

Minimalism inherently relies on letting go of items or space. Exactly how you tackle that will be different for each person. Obviously, if you are embarking on a van life adventure, you understand that the entire house or apartment cannot fit inside the van. Minimalism is the name of the game.

When living in a van, you'll have about 40 square feet, give or take, to put your items. That means consuming and purchasing mindfully. Deciding to keep or buy one item will inevitably mean forgoing another item.

Thinking of minimalism as a habit rather than a set of actions can help keep up with the clutter that you don't want building up in the van. Even when you purge most of your wardrobe, sell your furniture, and consolidate the rest of your belongings, that consumerist mindset can still kick in while on the road. To create a minimalist habit, practice not purchasing items when you visit a place—take pictures as your memories instead! Meal prepping and planning will help build the minimalist mindset, too. No need to buy rice vinegar "just to have it on hand," because that will take up valuable storage space in a van kitchen. Instead, plan out meals so you can use all the food in the van rather than rely on the long-term storage of most kitchens in homes or apartments. The habit of minimalism isn't built by doing one big purge. It is built by resisting the urge to add to your items time and time again.

If you need a list of essential items to get you started, try the following:

- A computer
- A phone
- Charging cords
- Two weeks worth of undergarments
- Capsule wardrobe
- Two plates, bowls, and sets of utensils
- One pan and one pot
- A week's worth of essential groceries
- Toiletries (toilet paper, deodorant, toothbrush, and toothpaste)

Your individual list may vary depending on your personal needs, but some variation of that sample list should be a good start for most people. There are ways to decorate the van and keep personal, significant items with you while still adhering to the minimalist habit. As you progress on this minimalist journey, you'll find that most of us keep much more than we need.

Chapter 2
Buying a Pre-Constructed Van

If the toolbox intimidates you, have no fear. Converting a van from scratch is not for everyone. There are plenty of options for purchasing pre-built vans. Most of the pre-built models will have a higher price tag than standard vans. Considering some van conversions can cost upwards of $10,000, the pre-built price tag may justify itself.

Pre-built vans are great options for van lifers taking on an auto loan to pay for their van, because an auto loan will not cover the conversion costs when purchasing a standard van. We will cover the basics of where and how to purchase a converted van, what key qualities to consider when touring a potential van, and how to easily make updates that don't require extensive handy work.

Where to Buy

There are several online marketplaces for purchasing pre-built vans, RVs, and school buses. The general online marketplaces like Facebook Marketplace or Craigslist are options, but these "for sale by owner" models are not always as reliable as the dedicated van and RV purchasing websites.

RVTrader is a great resource that I used when purchasing my first van. This website caters to van-hunters who want both new and used models. Search by year, model, or price point to get dozens of options. You can search by zip code, too, so only listings within a certain mileage of your home base will appear. Already driving across the country? You can search for parts and gear on RVTrader too. Once you've been on the road for a while and you want to change up your vehicle, you could use RVTrader to sell the van as well.

Van Life Trader is another online resource specifically geared towards buying and selling pre-built vans. If you are still considering van life, this site also offers van rentals via Outdoorsy. You can pick up a van near you, pay per day, and take a road trip to test out the van lifestyle.

If you want the same level of customization that is available when doing your own conversion, but you don't have the building skills to convert a van, then consider purchasing a custom van. Vanlife Customs.com allows customers to design their dream van and leave all the work to the crew at Van Life Custom. They have a streamlined process that includes a launch call, design meetings, and build updates. This option is exciting but expensive. It isn't the best process for a first-time van lifer, but once you've dedicated yourself to the lifestyle, then think of it as building a house. You want everything to be exactly to your liking and best suited to your lifestyle.

Non-negotiable Elements for the Best Deals

Every van conversion is built differently. Consider your non-negotiable features before you even start hunting. If you were building this van yourself, what would you need to include? Solar? Running water? Two beds? A workspace? Make sure that the pre-built vans you research and buy have the features that you need. We'll cover the updating process next, but updating isn't ideal. If you are trying to avoid the handiwork associated with converting the van yourself, then don't purchase a van that will need significant updates to be the quality of van you are looking for. This might mean spending a few extra dollars to get exactly what you want.

Making Updates

If you do have to make updates to the pre-built van that you purchase, be sure to consult with a professional handyman before attempting anything yourself. Everyone's situation is unique and these guidelines are meant to be broad, helpful pointers to get you started.

Always have a mechanic check out the van to make sure the engine and parts that are essential to travel work well. Technical repairs to breaks, transmissions, and engines are expensive and hard to coordinate once you are already on the road. If you do need to update any parts, get those fixed prior to beginning your journey.

Making interior updates is also possible. Consider whether or not the changes you want to make will involve dismantling any previously installed features. Electrical wiring, pipes, and lights are probably covered by insulation, so making those changes will be expensive and time-consuming. Layout changes are more attainable. If you want an additional foot of working space instead of kitchen space, that is an easy update.

Changes to design like the flooring, wall colors, and wood stains are also easy interior updates that you can make so that a pre-built van feels more personalized.

Chapter 3
Financing Life on the Road

If you are living out of a van, sleeping at a new camp spot every night, then you certainly aren't going into an office from nine to five every day. Most van lifers are working remotely, relying on passive income or running their own businesses. Even though life on the road is significantly cheaper than living in a house or an apartment, you'll still need some source of income.

Your Budget

Most van life budgets will look similar, but if you are running a business that requires its own unique supplies, that will affect your budget. Take advantage of the tools available to make budgeting easy. Some people rely on budgeting apps, while others prefer spreadsheets—and some even like the old-fashioned pen and paper method. Use whatever method works for you.

To begin, write down all of your guaranteed monthly expenses. If you purchased your van with an auto loan, then that loan payment is likely your largest expense. This list should include smaller payments, too, like cloud storage and streaming services. The others could be as follows:

- Loan payment
- Car insurance

How to Live the Van Life Dream

- Groceries
- Gas
- Phone bill
- Monthly subscriptions

Once you have an idea of the average amount of money going out the door every month, you can estimate how much you need to make in order to pay the bills, save, invest, and live comfortably. If you are working a full-time job remotely, then your monthly income won't fluctuate. In these situations, you can tailor your expenses to your income.

For freelancers, business owners, and passive income seekers, the month-to-month income may vary drastically. Of course, these jobs come with added flexibility, so there are trade-offs to be made on both ends of the job spectrum.

Some of your expenses will be harder to calculate each month, may not need to be paid each month, or maybe they can be paid one year at a time. These variable and long-term expenses can include:

- Campsite fees
- National parks passes
- Laundry
- Van maintenance
- Business expenses

Some expenses, like repairs to the van, cannot be anticipated, so you'll always want enough liquid cash to cover the unexpected. Depending on where you plan to spend most of your nights, you may need to pay campsite fees. If you want to avoid those fees, you can stay on public land or give urban camping a try, but we'll get into the details of where to park the van at night in Chapter 6.

If you are concerned about inflation and rising prices at the gas pump and grocery store, then try a few of these quick tips to save even more money on the road.

Tip #1: Pay down debt. If you still have student loans, medical bills, or credit card debt when you begin life on the road, then be sure to prioritize lowering your debt. Being debt-free is an amazing goal and brings a feeling of freedom. Plus, once those monthly payments on your debt burdens are gone, your budget will feel much roomier.

Tip #2: Test out different methods. Some budgeters like the 50/30/20 rule, where 50% of your budget covers necessary expenses, 30% is reserved for saving, and 20% is recreational money. Other people prefer something more granular, like the old mantra that housing shouldn't take up more than 30% of your monthly budget. Of course, housing takes on a whole new meaning when you are living on the road.

Tip #3: Revisit your budget every month. Your financial situation could be different each month, so don't hold yourself to the same standards month after month. If you drive more miles and need more gas one month, then don't beat yourself up about the extra gas. Budgeting shouldn't limit your lifestyle; it should flow with it. There's a difference between going over budget and changing a budget to fit your needs. Obviously, if you set a goal of only spending $45 per month on streaming services but impulsively subscribed to a new provider, then you've broken your budget. That is a different situation than realistically assessing how you did with your budget last month and what you need to change moving forward. Life in the van will bring you a new challenge every day, and your budget should reflect that flexibility.

Passive Income Tips and Opportunities

Need ideas for passive income opportunities and other non-traditional work options? You've come to the right place. I chose to run my business from a van. I also rely on investment properties, rented out, to bring in a steady stream of income. Your exact situation may look different than mine, but I'm passionate about helping people learn how to travel full-time and actively make money.

Passive income refers to income earned through ventures where the earner is not actively involved in the process. Investments in properties and limited partnerships are the only ventures that strictly qualify as passive income. Earnings from rental properties or businesses that are managed by others most of the time are also classified as passive income. However, side hustles, freelancing, or owning a personal business do not qualify as passive income. These kinds of income are considered active income and should be filed as such during tax season. It is important to note that although passive income is taxable, investments and dividend payments from portfolios are categorized as portfolio income and do not qualify as passive income when filing taxes. Therefore, it is crucial to understand the differences between these types of income when pursuing your van life dreams.

Let's briefly explore the different opportunities that are available to most people.

Real Estate Investing

Investing in real estate is one of the best returns for the money available today. It is easier than most people think, and you don't need to have tons of cash on hand to invest in real estate.

I recommend hunting for cheap houses in affordable cities. You don't need to focus only on real estate for sale in your base city. Since you'll be on the road most of the time, it doesn't matter if your rental property is in Ohio, Florida, or anywhere in between. Once you've gotten the hang of investing in real estate and earning passive income from renters, there's no limit to how many investment properties you can own. Of course, with more properties comes more responsibility, but these investments pay for themselves and are highly lucrative.

The money you earn from renters in your investment properties does count as passive income. I recommend hiring a property manager or management company to help run the day-to-day operation of the rental property. They will manage the renters and repairs and collect rent for a portion of the property's earnings. In exchange, you only need to check-in when there is a large-scale repair or a change in tenants. The property manager will free up your time to generate other sources of passive income or simply enjoy the world around you.

Section 8 Housing can be a great option for first-time real estate investors. This government-subsidized rent for low-income families guarantees the landlord receives their rent every month because the government is supplying part or all of the rental payment. Section 8 also tends to have less tenant turnover. Renters moving in and out of your property each year can add extra wear and tear to a house, making costs add up as you prepare to move in a new tenant and keeping you involved more often. To qualify for Section 8 renters, you'll need to complete an inspection process with the Department of Housing and Urban Development (HUD). This government department handles all Section 8 housing inquiries. Once you are approved, the renters come to you. Section 8 is a competitive market for renters, so getting your property approved in a city that has a long Section 8 waitlist should guarantee you a fast renting process.

Or, you could convert your investment property into an Airbnb property. Renting to vacationers on short- and long-term trips can be another great source of revenue. Remember that when leasing on Airbnb, as opposed to traditional renting, you'll need to have a fully furnished home for the guests. Take high-quality photos of your property and include a detailed introduction to yourself and the property; this will attract more renters. Some Airbnb policies, like cancellations and cleaning fees, have changed since the COVID-19 pandemic, so be sure to stay up to date on the things you'll be responsible for when choosing to rent the property through Airbnb.

E-Commerce

E-commerce refers to online businesses, and it includes dropshipping, affiliate marketing, Online Arbitrage, Amazon FBA, and other online business options. These businesses are easy to run from a van so long as you have a stable internet connection.

If you've never run a business before or have no idea where to start, there are a few platforms that make getting started in e-commerce, specifically dropshipping, easy. Shopify, and InventorySource all offer great programs for first-time e-commerce business owners. Dropshipping is an e-commerce structure that works especially well for van lifers. You don't need to worry about manufacturing or shipping any of the products yourself. In most dropshipping arrangements, you, as the e-commerce business owner, act as a middleman between a manufacturer that creates a product you support and the consumers who need an easy way to purchase that product online. Dropshippers create product pages, paywalls, and market products created by someone else. Once those steps are set up, you get to hop in the driver's seat and explore the world while the sales roll in.

Amazon allows anyone to start their own e-commerce profile. Not only do they make it simple to get started, but operating on Amazon's platform will make your company more reputable to potential consumers. Buyers trust Amazon, so with that brand behind you, the sales will increase. Fulfillment by Amazon (FBA) packages and ships the products for you. All you need to do is create an Amazon seller's account and start adding products to your account. There's a useful list of Amazon pre-approved products that you can rely on at first. You can sell restricted items, as well, but Amazon requires their sellers to follow strict rules if the products are on the restricted list. For every sale you make, Amazon receives a cut of the sales and you receive a cut of the sales.

Shopify is another e-commerce platform that is easy to use for first-time drop shippers. Whether you want to sell third-party products, like the Amazon opportunity, or sell your own original products, Shopify is a great option. They help you build an online store that looks professional and works similarly to web pages made with WordPress or Squarespace. Unlike Amazon, Shopify does require a monthly membership fee, and they won't handle the shipping process for you. When using Shopify, you'll need to be prepared to ship the products yourself or make that arrangement with the manufacturer.

Affiliate marketing is another online business model that can take your store or your simple blog to the next level. It is also entirely passive income, because you can earn while you sleep. Anyone can be an affiliate marketer. All you need is a blog, website, social media account, or newsletter to get started.

In affiliate marketing, creators and business owners partner with a company and promote that company's products. You'll attract an audience of buyers who then use your direct links to buy the company's products. Once a sale is made through your link, then you are paid a small cut of the purchase price by the company. It is a similar process to sales workers earning a commission. Most companies that work with affiliate marketers require your account to reach a minimum amount of money before they will payout.

Once again, there is an easy path to getting started with affiliate marketing through Amazon. But more stores than Amazon offer opportunities here. Brick and mortar stores like Target and Ulta also have affiliate marketing programs.

The easiest way to include affiliate marketing links in your online presence is to create product review videos, blogs, or posts. However you choose to include an affiliate link, make sure to include a disclaimer that you will profit from your followers using that link.

Creative Careers and Freelancing

This is a catch-all category of creative jobs, and freelancing opportunities do not qualify as passive income most of the time. Even though you won't be working a traditional nine to five, you will be actively working for the income you earn.

If you are artistically inclined, then consider starting an online store to sell your art. Multiple platforms offer an artistic, online marketplace where creators sell paintings, pottery, graphic designs, and more. Etsy, RedBubble, and Society 6 are all great options that work in slightly different ways. For example, if you are a physical artist, then Etsy is the best option for you. Artists can set up their own store page, create product pages, and sell their art. But, the artist is responsible for the shipping of the products. You receive a higher cut of the purchase price because the shipping is your responsibility. On the other hand, RedBubble and Society 6 are better suited for digital designs and art. Just like Etsy, you'll create an account, online store, and product pages. Here is where the platforms differ. On RedBubble and Society 6, you select what products you want your designs printed on, then the platform manufactures that product and design, and the platform handles all the shipping. Because RedBubble and Society 6 do so much work for the artists, the cut you receive is smaller, but when working and living from a van with limited space, that sacrifice may be worth it.

If you aren't artistically inclined but you are good with words, then you should consider ghostwriting to earn money while you're living in the van. Ghostwriters write manuscripts, blogs, and articles for clients who have content ideas but lack the skills to write the manuscripts themselves.

To get started in ghostwriting, set up an online portfolio that you can connect to your LinkedIn and share when applying for jobs. The best platforms for creating an online portfolio include Squarespace and Copyfolio. They have free and paid options for whatever fits your budget. Finding clients organically may take time, so create profiles on freelance websites, too. Sites like Upwork, Fiverr, and Workana are popular for ghostwriters and freelancers of all kinds. These platforms allow freelancers to set their rates, apply for posted jobs, and pitch their services. Each of the platforms takes a cut of the final pay for each position, but the cuts they take will depend on the number of jobs you've completed and the cost of the current job.

If you are more inclined to edit the written word than write it, then there are opportunities for you too! Editors and proofreaders can also create profiles on freelance websites and find work editing and proofreading clients' manuscripts, blogs, and articles. Some companies will even hire freelance editors to help them with their internal and external-facing documents. These opportunities are great for contract work arrangements wherein the worker contracts with a company for a set amount of time or a set amount of deliverables. Once that work has been finished, the worker is free to move on to another project and company.

Some lesser-known creative pursuits like ghost-producing and creating courses online are also fun options that allow you to earn income from your passions. Ghost-producing is far less understood than ghostwriting, but it works in similar ways. Ghost-producers create tracks for musicians and artists to buy and use on their songs and albums. Some of the most popular artists in the world rely on ghost producers to help them create their music, so ghost-producing follows strict non-disclosure agreements. Music fans would be horrified if they learned their favorite artist wasn't really the genius behind their best song. Ghost-producers can upload their work to websites like affordableghostproduction.com and find clients looking for their music.

Maybe you want to create an online course for the hobbies you have mastered. There are platforms that facilitate course creation for beginners, like Teachable, but you can also add your course as paid content on a website you've already established. If you are an artist, you could create an art course; if you are a writer, you could create a creative writing class. People will pay for courses to better their investment skills, learn a language, pick up a new hobby, you name it!

Influencer Marketing

Social media influencers may seem like minor celebrities, and some of them have developed to celebrity status, but they all started as average social media users just like you and me. The difference between your Instagram which has 300 followers and an influencer's following of 10 million is work.

Influencer marketing is a subtle and influential way that companies use to get their products in front of consumers. Most influencers must work their way up the social ladder and build a small following of their own before being contacted by a brand. Creators find and create a niche or community. Once established, brands and companies will come to them. They ask popular creators to promote their products. This can include posting a certain number of content pieces about the product, posting full-length videos, or writing blog articles. In return, the influencer gets to sample products, earn a paycheck, and grow their following. The compensation normally depends on the amount of content desired.

How to Live the Van Life Dream

When just getting started in influencer marketing, you'll need to find your niche. Some topics like beauty and pets are overcrowded online communities. It is easier to be a big fish in a small pond than a small fish in a big pond. The more specific you can get, the better. I call it niching down. If you are an avid outdoorsman who wants to work in influencer marketing in the outdoor gear community, don't just stop at outdoor gear. Pick a specific activity, like fishing. Get even more specific from there: Do you like freshwater fishing or ocean fishing? Fly fishing or traditional hooks? These tiny details can be the difference between earning a brand deal or not. If a company doesn't think you fit their product well enough, they'll find a dozen others who do.

Some platforms like Collabfluence help match new social media figures with companies who want to give influencer marketing a try. For an influencer who is just starting out, this option is very helpful. After a few deals, the bigger companies will find you.

Remember that all social media platforms use algorithms, so you'll need to use the right hashtags, follow the right accounts, and be active every day to make the algorithm work in your favor.

Most social media influencers also rely on blogs and websites to connect with followers. Here, you can add longer-form content and collate all your information in one place. These sites are also great opportunities to generate some extra income. Installing Cost Per Click (CPC) ads can generate significant revenue, especially if you tailor these ads towards the kind of content you create. If you are showcasing van life on your social media and blog, then your CPC ads should focus on outdoor gear, vacations, and automotive products. Keep everything in line with your niche and you will see greater success. CPS ads will pay hosts based on the number of clicks the ad gets, so the more followers and users you can direct to the ads, the better.

You can check out my other book, *The Ultimate Van Life Guide to Passive Income*, for a detailed look at all the different passive income opportunities available, how to invest smartly, start your own business, and work smarter not harder while on the road.

Chapter 4
The Big Bathroom Questions

One of the most common questions that prospective van lifers have is, "How do you live in a van full-time without a bathroom?" And the answer to this question differs depending on who you ask.

In Chapter 1, we discussed plumbing installation. For most van lifers who opt to equip the van with running water, this setup is only for a sink and drinking water, not a full bathroom. But there are solutions for having a bathroom in the van as well as options for finding facilities when you don't have a bathroom on board.

If your van life vehicle of choice is an RV, then you will likely have a full bathroom on board with a waste tank that can be emptied at the proper stations. Or, if you have found and converted a school bus, then you may have the extra space to install a formal bathroom on board. For most, but not all, van lifers in standard Sprinter vans, there simply isn't the room for a toilet and shower within 40 square feet. Some van lifers have gotten creative with their bathroom setups and we'll share their fantastic ideas.

Bathroom Options

The bathroom solution you choose will depend on the lifestyle you want to have on the road. For some people, planning their trip around the next public restroom or using the great outdoors as their toilet isn't within their comfort level. But, remember that creating a bathroom solution within your van comes with a cost both to your wallet and your space.

Wet Bath

A wet bath is the most private and formal type of shower and toilet combination that you can install within a van. Per the name, a wet bath is built so that all the surfaces can be wet. They are made with tile, just like traditional restrooms, only smaller. These setups provide the most privacy of any option. They can be used at a moment's notice.

Most wet baths look like a closet from the outside, but when opened they reveal a tiled chamber with a toilet and a showerhead. They are very small: Imagine a room smaller than even a stall shower in a locker room. They include both the toilet seat and the showerhead. When installing plumbing, van lifers who choose this option will need extra piping to connect the showerhead to the water tank and extra pipes for connecting the drain to the gray tank. This could also be a great place to consider the hole drilled in the floor method that we discussed in Chapter 1.

Weight is the most important consideration when building a true wet bath in your van. Waterproofing materials are heavy and you want to decrease the weight of this build as much as possible. Aluminum shower pans can be a great resource to reduce weight.

Hybrid Bath

A hybrid bath is one of the best options for van lifers who desperately want the convenience of a bathroom on board but may not have the space or materials to build out a full wet bath.

Hybrid baths make use of hidden shelves or trap doors that reveal a shower. They aren't watertight like a wet bath, or as private. However, these bathroom facilities are great for multi-use space. In most cases, the toilet is visible in a corner of the van, then you could remove a drain cover, drop down a curtain, and open a cabinet to reveal a showerhead.

This option is easy to use, easier to build than a wet bath, and cheaper. Be mindful when laying out the van that the cabinets or furniture pieces around the hybrid bath may get splashed. It is best not to keep your workstation, with laptops and papers, right next to the hybrid bath.

No Bath

Forgetting the toilet and shower on board the van entirely is a surprisingly common design choice. Van lifers, like myself, without an onboard bathroom must rely on public bathrooms or nature as their toilet.

However, the showering consideration has some interesting solutions. The best, and most underrated option, is to purchase a premium Planet Fitness membership or comparable gym membership. Planet Fitness has locations all across the United States. Every gym has a large bathroom with shower stalls for members to clean up after a workout—or, for van lifers to drop in and shower off when they are nearby. For $24.99 per month, members have unlimited access to every gym in the country.

If you are planning on staying further off the grid than the nearest Planet Fitness, then this option may not be best for your unique travel plans.

For those relying on nature as a toilet when you camp off-grid, make sure to dispose of all toiletries properly. Not only is littering bad for the environment, but the smell of used bathroom materials can also attract wild animals as you sleep at night. Most outdoor sporting stores sell sealable containers for wipes, menstrual products, and hygiene products. Looking for even better bathroom gadgets? Online stores sell silicon urine funnels and solar showers that can hang from a tree and spout water. Thanks to these products, living off the grid doesn't have to be a hygienic sacrifice.

Chapter 5
Internet and Other Technology

Getting internet on the road is another primary question that prospective van lifers ask all the time. Wi-Fi is essential, especially for those who work remotely or run a business from the road. It is also nice to have for checking email, streaming movies, or running a GPS.

We'll dive into the best options for Wi-Fi on the road, and once you have picked the system that works for your lifestyle, you should look into the top apps for van lifers. These apps can make life easier and enhance the van life experience.

Getting Internet on the Road

There are several products on the market that can help you use the internet while on the road. Some of them operate very similarly to traditional Wi-Fi. Others simply make your van a data hot spot. We'll review some of the most popular options for most van lifers.

Unlimited Cellular Data

Unlimited data sounds like an expensive luxury to non van lifers, but once you've cut out monthly expenses like rent, utilities, and Wi-Fi by jumping into van life full time, you should have the room in your budget for unlimited data. Many cellular companies already make unlimited data a standard package, so maybe you already pay for this feature!

Use a signal booster to improve the reception your phone receives. Boosters can run the GPS, help you work remotely, and allow you to stream videos without lags or endless loading. When tethering your laptop to a hot spot and booster, some phone carriers limit the amount of data you can use.

Metered connections will make your data last longer. They limit background updates and other functions that suck data.

Shop around for the best deals and coverage. Not every unlimited plan is the same. Consider what areas of the country you'll be in frequently. If your van life will be taking you off the grid frequently, then don't buy from a phone carrier that prioritizes coverage in cities.

Starlink

Starlink, a satellite-based internet service provided by SpaceX, is a promising new option for users worldwide seeking high-speed internet coverage. For van lifers, this means the exciting opportunity to stay connected on the go. The service involves a small satellite dish and modem that can provide internet access from virtually anywhere, with better results found in the Western Half of the United States.

Many van lifers opt to buy the Residential Starlink and use "roaming" to gain prioritized connection. The service has also released a new version that lets users connect while driving, expanding connectivity options.

However, the service does have some disadvantages. While the internet speed is impressive, disruptions during bad weather and high costs may make it unaffordable for some van lifers. Additionally, a clear view of the sky is necessary, meaning that areas with obstructions such as trees or mountains may not provide an optimal connection.

Overall, Starlink is a great option for those van lifers who prioritize staying connected, but it may not be the most suitable option for everyone due to its limitations and high cost.

Insty Connect

Insty Connect is a company that offers an internet solution for people living in vans or RVs. Their service provides high-speed internet access, with a reliable connection that allows van lifers to stay connected to the internet no matter where they are. The main advantage of using Insty Connect is that it provides reliable internet access, which is essential for many people who live and work on the road. With a stable connection, van lifers can stream videos, work online, or keep in touch with loved ones through social media.

However, there are a few disadvantages of using Insty Connect. Firstly, their service can be quite expensive, which may not be feasible for those on a tight budget. Additionally, their coverage may not be available in some areas, which means that there may be times when van lifers have limited access to the internet. Nevertheless, Insty Connect is an excellent choice for those who need a reliable and high-speed internet connection on the road.

MiFi

MiFi devices are mobile Wi-Fi hotspots that allow roughly 15GB of data per month. Some models offer slightly more or slightly less data. These devices can be purchased from most major phone carriers like Verizon. As our mobile technology improves, some MiFi devices can even get 5G data, just like the newest phones.

Using a MiFi is best when used in combination with unlimited cellular data. If your work requires you to upload and download images or videos frequently, then you will use your data faster than others. Jobs that aren't heavy on images and videos should see this as the best option.

A few phone carriers let customers add a MiFi device to their monthly phone bill. You can expect to pay $5 to $25 per month from most major carriers, plus the cost of the device itself. Vreizon in particular has a good plan for MiFi devices and unlimited data. The exact coverage will depend on the carrier.

Boosters

Signal boosters will increase the speed of your internet. They allow calls and texts to go through more reliably no matter where you are. You can buy boosters from third-party retailers like Amazon or Walmart. You can also purchase them directly through your phone company.

There are extremely cheap boosters on the market and extremely expensive ones. Read reviews before you decide what to purchase. As far as the boosters are concerned, spending a few extra dollars adds a lot of value.

Boosters do require cell phone data or Wi-Fi to work. These devices don't create an internet connection. They make it stronger. Don't rely only on a booster for your internet and data. Instead, you can buy a booster if you are struggling with your current connection.

Finding Free Internet

If you will be living in the van near urban areas, then you may be able to skip the boosters, MiFi, and phone data altogether. Relying on public Wi-Fi from coffee shops, stores, and libraries might be able to get the job done.

Sometimes, relying on free internet isn't truly 'free.' Coffee shops will require you to purchase food or drink to sit in the shop and do your work. This setup doesn't sound so bad until you are buying six $5 iced coffees a week. Libraries are better for internet that is truly free, and they offer great community spaces where you could meet the locals.

Hopping from free Wi-Fi network to free Wi-Fi network won't be a good option if you were hoping to get away from the cities on your van life adventure. It will also mean you are stuck with your standard phone data when it comes to running items like the GPS or making calls.

The Best Apps

Once you've chosen the best internet solution for your van life plans, you should check out the following apps to take your travels to the next level.

How to Live the Van Life Dream

These apps cover a range of uses from community builders to enhanced GPS systems. Even when you close the door on renting or owning a home in favor of the van, you aren't leaving everything behind. Your phone is probably following you everywhere you go, so make the most of it!

The Van Life App

The Van Life app was an app created for van lifers by van lifers. This app brings the van community together so life on the road doesn't have to be lonely. It is first and foremost a resource app. Van lifers leave messages about cheap gas, free campsites, and tips or tricks they've learned on the message boards. It has also become a way of literally bringing together the van life community. You can coordinate where you'll be camping, what routes you're driving, and more to meet people doing the same thing you are: exploring our beautiful world from the comfort of their van. Users can 'connect' with each other and send direct messages, so it is easy to plan meetups.

Van Life is free and works on both Apple and Android products. It does need cell service to function.

AllTrails

AllTrails is a popular app for hikers and nature lovers. While not all van lifers are nature lovers, the two do tend to go hand in hand. Having an app to help find the best hiking trails and sights will make your van life adventure even more attainable and picturesque. It will show you a map of the trail, give a difficulty rating, and show pictures of the area. The app allows you to filter results based on location, elevation, and even views.

Users can upgrade their AllTrails app to the Pro model which allows the maps and information to be accessed even without cell service. The upgraded features cost $2.50/month or $29.99/year. If you are planning to adventure deep into national parks or public land, then upgrading to Pro may be a cost worth budgeting for. AllTrails is available for Apple and Android products. It also works on a desktop.

GasBuddy

Gas expenses can add up quickly. Many van lifers rely on GasBuddy to help them find the cheapest fuel. The app finds the best deals on gas and diesel near your current location. It is always frustrating to pay for fuel and discover a cheaper station 10 miles down the road. Thankfully, GasBuddy eliminates that problem. Even if you are just saving a few cents by using the app, those cents add up over time.

The app has upgraded recently with new features like GasBack which allows you to pay at the pump via the app and earn rewards points that can be redeemed at future fill-ups. They have added a trip cost calculator so you can estimate how much you'll spend on gas throughout your road trip, and a vehicle recall page to stay up to date on your vehicle's health.

The app is free and it works on both Apple and Android devices.

US Public Lands

Whoever told you there is no such thing as free has clearly never heard of public land. You can camp on public land for free! The US Public Lands App displays where the public land—Bureau of Land Management—is on a map so you can camp with confidence that you aren't encroaching on private land or paid campsites.

You can't specifically see where to camp on this public land, but having a visual of the public land area takes one step out of the stressful process of finding somewhere to sleep. There are more than 247 million acres of public land in this country, so the odds you'll pass through it are high!

The US Public Lands app is $2.99, an easy price to pay for the incredible value it can provide for your van life experience.

Waze

Waze is a GPS app that goes beyond the basic direction capabilities you expect from a GPS. This app also alerts you to traffic, tolls, police speed traps, and construction, and it shows you the other Waze users on the road around you. This app is incredibly helpful to van lifers who might want to find the road less traveled. If you are trying to save money, then using the app to avoid costly tolls is another perfect use.

Waze is free and it works on both Apple and Android devices.

Harvest Hosts

Harvest Hosts is an innovative app that provides road trippers and van lifers with exclusive access to thousands of unique and exciting camping spots that are not available anywhere else.

With this app, camping enthusiasts can enjoy once-in-a-lifetime experiences and exciting amenities that they would not find at traditional campsites. To book their stays, van lifers will need to plan their route and reserve their spots in advance. Membership and hosting options are available for an annual fee. Harvest Hosts is free to download and accessible on both Apple and Android devices.

Harvest Host has been an absolute game changer for us. It has truly made our Van Life experience a trip of a lifetime. We have stayed at countless farms, bowling alleys, golf courses, wineries, the list is endless. It's a must have for anyone wanting unique experiences all over the United States.

Chapter 6
Go to Sleep Without Counting Sheep

One of your top priorities should be finding a safe place to sleep. We will cover the two main options: urban camping and rural camping. If you plan to stay close to urban areas while living in the van, then you will spend many nights urban camping. Meanwhile, van lifers who want to get off the grid will need to book campsites or find public land where they can spend the night.

Both of these options come with their advantages and disadvantages, and whichever one you choose will reflect the adventure you hope to have. There are some basic safety concerns that apply in both situations.

For example, make sure to purchase high-quality window covers and windshield covers so no one can see in the van at night. You can find these through online retailers like Amazon and some brick-and-mortar auto stores. Try to find blackout-grade curtains. These will block out the light from street lamps if you are urban camping or block out the rising sun on early mornings when you'd rather sleep in. You also need to invest in a locked safe. You can put your valuables, like passports, documents, cash, and jewelry in the safe whenever you are away from the van. Most safes are combination locked, but you can find models that lock with a key or pin code if you prefer those methods.

The van will have standard locks and a standard alarm system, but consider purchasing extra locks for additional security, especially if you are traveling alone. If you purchased an older, used van, it may not have a panic button. Make sure to have a mechanic install a new panic alarm before you hit the road.

Shop around for first aid kits and small vehicle repair bags that include jumper cables, a flashlight, tools to change a tire, and hazard flags. Details like these are often the ones that people forget most often but always list during their "things I wish I knew" stories.

If you are traveling with a pet—or even if you aren't—consider putting a "beware of dog" sign on the back window of the van. Dogs are often one of the biggest deterrents to would-be thieves or burglars; no one wants to risk getting a bite from an animal. Consider buying your dog an LED collar, as well. If Fido has to go to the bathroom while you are at a campsite, you want to be able to keep track of them as the sun is setting. Some dogs can be spooked by noises and bark until the sun comes up. CBD calming treats can decrease your dog's anxiety and keep them sleeping peacefully all night.

Some van lifers prefer to have a defense weapon on board the van when they are traveling and sleeping. Smaller protective devices like pepper spray or pocket knives can be good ideas, especially if you are traveling alone. Larger-scale protective devices like guns or tasers come with a new set of considerations. Not every state has the same gun laws, so crossing state lines with that kind of weapon could get you in legal trouble. If you do plan on bringing a gun with you, make sure to do thorough research on the gun laws of every state you plan to visit. And, look into the rules for any national parks on your list. Most national parks do not allow firearms within the grounds.

No matter which camping environment you find yourself in, always use common sense. If your gut is telling you that something feels off, relocate. Make your final bathroom break if there isn't a bathroom in the van before it gets dark out, and avoid leaving the van for any reason in the middle of the night.

Urban Camping

Whether you plan on adventuring into nature or staying close to cities, you will inevitably spend a few nights urban camping, or stealth camping, in a parking lot or on a street. I have even spent my fair share of nights sleeping in a parking lot, so I can share my best tips for safe areas and silent nights.

My favorite parking lot camping spots were Cabelas, Cracker Barrel, Planet Fitness, and Buc-ee's (when they allowed parking lot camping). All of these establishments were safe, public areas to spend the night.

Wherever you end up parking for the night, make sure there are other cars around, well-lit streets, and easy routes out of the area in case you start to feel unsafe.

Some van lifers recommend parking in neighborhood streets to sleep when urban camping. These locations can be safe and easy, but be sure you aren't parking in a spot that requires special, city parking passes. Or, if you are in a suburban area, be sure that the neighborhood you've chosen isn't gated or a part of a homeowner's association (HOA). These neighborhoods might feel very safe, but they don't want van lifers parking on their streets, either.

Rural Camping

For those of you who plan to spend most of your time away from the cities and deep into nature, you'll be rural camping. This camping style includes public land, national parks, campsites, and backcountry adventures. You won't have the same safety concerns as van lifers who chose urban camping, but there are still important considerations for camping out in the wild.

Public lands will not be set up like traditional campgrounds. Some but not all are free and have specific borders. The US Public Lands app we discussed earlier can help you identify the areas designated as public land or managed by the Bureau of Land Management. You can remain for up to 14 consecutive days on BLM land. After those 14 days, the BLM requests that campers travel at least 25 miles from the site so as not to hurt the natural resources there. They also request that personal belongings not be left unattended for more than 10 days in a row.

Whenever you enter a campground, make sure to find the park ranger on duty and introduce yourself. If your campsite neighbor doesn't give you a good feeling, then switch campsites before turning in for the night. You can never be too careful. Make sure you have a map of the park so you know where to go if you need anything. Motion sensor lights can be a great security feature if you are camping in campgrounds or on public lands. If your van is the only vehicle or camping set up around, it could seem like an easy target.

Most national parks, especially the popular ones, require reservations ahead of time to use their campsites. We will cover more in-depth details about passes and restrictions in the next section. In general, national and state park campsites have more amenities than generic campgrounds or public land. Some can include grills, charging stations, and fire pits. Campgrounds of any nature may have public use showers and restrooms, too, so if there isn't a bathroom on board the van, you can use this opportunity to get cleaned up.

One of the perks of camping off the grid or in campgrounds is that you can stretch out of the van in ways that urban camping doesn't allow for. If you've brought lawn chairs or any outdoor activities, you can set those up around your campsite. Truly enjoy being out in nature, since that is likely what you left your house or apartment to do!

Community is another perk of staying in campgrounds and public land. If you are staying in an area for multiple days to adventure, hike, and work, then you can make connections with fellow van lifers passing through the area and other campers. The Van Life app we covered earlier is commonly used to organize group camping spots. Isolation and loneliness are two common misconceptions that outsiders have about van life. Of course, you'll have endless independence if that is your goal. But, you can also build a community of like-minded individuals and enjoy camping in the same spots together.

Passes and Restrictions

Not all campgrounds will be free. Do your research ahead of time to make sure you've paid your campsite fees and reserved a space. The last thing you want to do is pull up to the campground just to be told they're full. Some thought ahead planning is still necessary, even when living in the van.

If you want to explore the national parks, then purchasing an Annual Parks Pass will save you tons of time and money. The parks pass doesn't guarantee free camping within the parks, but most pass holders get a serious discount on the campsite rentals. Once purchased, all of your entrance fees are paid for the year, no matter how many parks you visit.

Most states have similar passes for their state parks. If you have one state you plan on exploring more than others, purchasing one of these annual state park passes is another great idea for extra camping and hiking options. Some states, like Texas, have more than 50 state parks. There's no shortage of beautiful land to explore.

Chapter 7
Van Life Hacks and Tips You Didn't Consider

Even the best planners don't remember every detail. That is why I've compiled this list of the lifestyle changes no one remembers to plan for while they live in a van. Most van lifers remember to ask about bathrooms, showers, and camping arrangements. Many forget that they will need to do laundry, stay active, and care for pets.

These are my proven tips and tricks learned from long trips in the van.

Laundry

Laundry can be one of those chores you take for granted. In a house or apartment, you probably have a full-sized washing machine and a dryer for your dozens of pieces of clothing. In the van, not only will you not have laundry machines, you also won't have as many clothes. A full wardrobe would take up too much space!

Van lifers typically cut down their wardrobe to the essentials:

- a few weeks' worth of underwear
- athleisure and hiking apparel
- pajamas and loungewear
- casual clothes

Other tips for cutting down on your laundry turnover—because even with these laundry solutions, you won't want to be worrying about washing clothes multiple times per week—include the following:

Rewear your clothes. Wearing a shirt or a pair of pants one time does not necessarily mean it is dirty. Unless you spilled something on your clothes or sweated excessively, you can wear that t-shirt more than once.

Speaking of t-shirts, try to transition from t-shirts to tank tops. T-shirts can get tight around the armpits, stained by deodorant, or smell faster than tank tops that avoid the armpit region. You'll get more wear per wash out of a tank top than a t-shirt.

Don't mix your active clothes with your casual clothes. The clothes you wear to hike, climb, swim, or do anything outside should be dedicated for that purpose. If you have to rewear those pieces, continue wearing them only for 'dirty' outdoor activities. This system will keep your casual clothes cleaner and fresher longer.

All of these wardrobe tips will keep you away from laundry day, but when the time to wash your clothes inevitably rolls around, these are the tips I recommend most. Most van lifers end up washing their clothes once a month, give or take. Really, this process is all about your personal preferences. If dirty clothes are your pet peeve, then you will end up dedicating more time and road trip directions looking for laundry solutions. If you are comfortable in some worn-twice-this-week tops, then you can stretch out the laundry schedule.

Laundromats are the most obvious choice for van lifers who want a traditional solution to doing laundry on the road. Laundromats are communal laundry facilities that require customers to pay per load. They were extremely common in big cities, many years ago. While less common now, they are still in operation all across the country. Looking for the best laundromat experience? Don't do your laundry on the weekends; that is when laundromats are most crowded. Bring your own detergent rather than relying on detergent you can purchase from the laundromat. And, make sure to wipe down the inside of a machine before you use it.

If you don't want to do all your laundry at a public facility, then investing in a portable washing machine is a great option for van life. These come in all shapes and sizes, and most of these portable machines can be purchased from online retailers like Amazon. They range in price from $60 to $275.

Mini and single tub washers can be great solutions for small loads of laundry. They weigh around 10 pounds and take up about as much space as a laundry hamper. Some models even function as a dryer once they've been cleared of wastewater.

Looking for an even smaller solution? Try portable washing machines. These small devices can be added to the side of any container of water, like a bucket or a plugged sink. To do a small load of laundry, you add water, detergent, and clothes to the container, then plug in the portable washing machine. The device will oscillate water in the container just like a washing machine. These devices are available through online retailers like Amazon, and they are typically less than $30.

Staying Active

Exercise is key to a happy, healthy lifestyle. This routine shouldn't stop just because you are living in the van. True, you won't have the same floor space to do a full at-home tabata routine, but there are still solutions for staying active while living full-time from the van.

Planet Fitness

If you purchased a premium Planet Fitness membership for the showers, then you have a built-in exercise option. There are 2,000 Planet Fitness locations in the United States, so you are likely never far from a workout and a soothing shower.

These gyms have cardio and strength equipment, plus room to stretch and practice bodyweight exercises. No matter what you love to do for exercise, you can find a solution inside Planet Fitness. They offer classes to their premium members, too, so you can meet people and follow an instructor if that is how you prefer to workout.

Other benefits of this gym's premium membership are the members only amenities like tanning, massages, and other relaxing therapies. Sitting in a driver's seat all day can make your muscles sore. What better way to relax than a hydromassage before a HIIT class?

Outdoor Activities

If one of your motivations for pursuing van life is the ability to get out in nature, then you have a built-in opportunity for staying active. Hiking, swimming, rock climbing, and whatever else you love to do outside is great exercise!

When you purchase a National Parks Annual Pass, you will have access to hundreds of hiking trails. Some trails, like Angels Landing at Zion National Park, are strenuous enough to leave you sore for days.

After several weeks of hiking and exploring the great outdoors, you could end up in the best shape of your life, all because you decided to start living in a van. Trend dieters won't believe it!

Yoga

Need to stay in the van on a rainy day? Are you urban camping in a Bucee's parking lot? That doesn't need to mean sacrificing your exercise routine for the day! Yoga is a great way to stay active inside the van. You should have room to practice all your yoga poses in the center walkway of the van.

To get the most out of your yoga routine, clear your mind. Does that sound easier said than done? Here are some tips for finding inner peace while you stretch, pose, and breathe.

First of all, actually breathe. Regular breathing, in through your nose and out through your mouth, will help slow your heart rate and give you something to focus on besides the constant chatter in your brain. Whenever you lose focus, return to thinking about your breathing. Thinking through the physical feelings in your body can help you focus, too. What does your foot feel like on the mat? Where is the tension in your body? In which muscles do you feel a stretch?

Most yoga teachers also recommend setting an intention for your practice. This intention should be focused on how you'll feel during your yoga practice, not on an end result. Intentions can vary, but they shouldn't be competitive goals. Center your intention around a connection to your body. Focus on a moral characteristic like gratitude or calm.

Set the mood if it helps you get in the right headspace. Turn down the lights in the van, light a candle if you have one, and put on some soothing, ambient music. These little details can make the difference between a distracted, strenuous practice and a restful experience.

You can find basic guides to yoga poses and how to do them properly from online videos and guides. Some of the basics you'll first encounter include sun salutation, downward dog, and warrior.

Cooking

Your van kitchen will not include many of the luxuries of a typical kitchen, like a full-sized stove, microwave, or refrigerator. There is also much less storage space in a van life kitchen. Never fear: None of these restrictions mean you'll have to sacrifice healthy meals. You can learn how to cook healthy meals in a small space.

Layouts and Appliances

First, let's go over the best kitchen layouts. In a van, you need to plan for efficiency. Most van kitchens will run along one of the side walls. Taller van lifers who need their beds to be oriented lengthwise may build their kitchens in the back corner of the van. Either way, there won't be more than four feet of counter space. If you have set up the plumbing in the van, you'll have a sink taking up some of your counter space, too.

Home chefs may want to get creative with their conversions to give them extra cooking space. Consider installing fold-out counters. These extra feet of counter space can be folded up when you are driving, sleeping, or doing anything besides cooking. When the van is in park and it is time to make breakfast or dinner, you can unfold these counters. Many van lifers build the counters so the extendable section crosses in front of the door or stretches through the width of the van to create an 'L' shaped cooking space. These extendable counters could be used as an extra desk or working space when you aren't moving, too!

Mini fridges may scream college dorm at first, but they are also useful in van kitchens. For vans with electricity, installing a mini fridge is a cost and space you'll want to plan for. Most mini fridges can be purchased from brick-and-mortar stores as well as from online retailers like Amazon. They cost between $100 and $200, but you can easily spend more depending on your needs and space.

For cooking hot meals, you'll probably rely on a hot plate or electric skillet. Hot plates and skillets can normally hold one or two pans at a time. They won't be as high-powered as a traditional stove, but they still get your food cooked in the end. If you are spending the extra dollar on your conversion, then you can install a small stovetop in the van. Some van lifers who love to cook and have the space have designed beautiful kitchens that include electric stoves. These are far less common than van lifers relying on hot plates.

Tools

Remember that whatever you store on shelves or in cabinets is liable to shift as you drive, hit bumps, and slam on the brakes. Most of the dishes and cookware you purchase should be plastic to avoid broken glass and ceramic crashing to the floor of the van.

Because you won't have the same storage space that you are used to relying on when you lived in a house or apartment, you'll want to keep only one or two of each of your dishes. Of course this depends on how many people you are traveling with. Two people in a van will inevitably need extra dishes. If you are traveling by yourself, however, then one dish, one bowl, and one set of utensils will get you through the day.

When buying your tools, try to buy multipurpose items. Tupperware bowls that double as salad and cereal dishes are useful. Shop for pots with built-in strainers or multi-use cups and travel cups that can hold hot and cold drinks.

Multi-use cookware is convenient not only for space but also for the cleanup after a meal. When you only have the water in your tank to work with, you won't want to waste it on washing a dozen dishes. You'll go through the water quickly washing that many dishes, and if you don't have an electric pump, then your hand or foot will get tired of pumping that much water.

Buy products that reduce waste, too. A full trash can will make the entire van smell, fast. Rather than single-use cleaning supplies like paper towels, try cleaning up messes with rags and aprons that can be washed and reused. The same goes for dish soap, sponges, and surface cleaners. You need a clean kitchen station without a pile of used Clorox wipes. Home remedies like baking soda and vinegar or homemade soaps can reduce the space and clutter of other cleaning supplies. Plus, they won't pile up the way single-use products will fill a trash bag.

Foods and Meal Prep

Grocery shopping when you live in a van requires lots of planning ahead. Some van lifers swear by meal prepping and planning, while others prefer to cook every day. No matter which you choose, you'll need to make room for the basic ingredients like spices and oils. Van life doesn't mean settling for flavorless food!

Ready-to-cook items rather than raw meat or raw rice and beans can really elevate your van life meals. These items still need to be heated or 'cooked' but they require much less preparation than their raw counterparts. Ready-to-cook meats like sausages or preseasoned chicken also help keep your kitchen sanitary. Raw meat, especially raw chicken, requires extra separation of ingredients and extra cleaning steps that are difficult to maintain in such a small space.

Some van lifers choose to experiment with vegetarianism or plant-based diets while they are on the road. It isn't a requirement of van life to give up meat, but it can make your cooking life easier. There are hundreds of delicious plant-based recipes like veggie burgers, burrito bowls, and sandwiches that will keep you full and fueled. A plant-based diet doesn't have to mean eating salads for every meal of the day.

Don't forget the snacks just because you are living in a van! You will need snacks to fuel you throughout the day whether you are driving or hiking through a national park. The best snacks will be healthy and space-friendly. As many items as you can keep out of the small mini fridge, the better.

Shop smart. When you are buying food, think about the next time you'll be near a grocery store. You need to balance space and time. If you are camping in rural areas and national parks, you may be far from the nearest grocery or convenience store for weeks on end. However, buying in bulk is likely not an option inside the confines of a van kitchen. Make your meals with ingredients that can be used in multiple dishes, rely on leftovers to the extent that you can, and don't overindulge in ingredients that take up a ton of space. Watermelon is a delicious fruit, but you won't have space for a whole watermelon in a mini fridge. Think of your meal planning this way: If you buy a red pepper, you could use half that pepper in a fajita dish one night and the other half in a stir-fry dish the next. Multi-use ingredients, like that red pepper, ensure that you aren't buying dozens of pieces of produce for your week's meals.

Need coffee while you're on the road? Never fear; there are multiple solutions for getting that caffeine fix in the van. Besides the jugs of cold brew that most grocery stores now sell, you can try making your own cold brew at home, as long as you have a jug and a filter, and store it in the mini fridge. No special equipment required! Start by filling a pitcher or jug with cold water. Next, add the proportionate amount of coffee to a reusable filter; for a 24 ounce pitcher, I would recommend 10 tablespoons of coffee. You can find reusable filters at most grocery stores or online. Place the filter inside the jug and allow it to steep in the fridge for 12 to 24 hours. When it is ready to drink, remove the filter, throw away the used coffee grounds, and enjoy. Cold brew made at home like this will have a robust flavor and a higher caffeine concentration than the store-bought coffee, and it is also customizable. You can make cold brew with your favorite beans, add other flavors, and pour over the milk of your choice.

If you prefer hot coffee but don't want to store a whole coffee pot in your limited kitchen space, then invest in a percolator or Italian press. These coffee makers don't require electricity; instead, they are heated over a stove, hot plate, or fire if you are truly camping. They are easy to clean, make coffee in small batches, and are small for storage needs.

Pets

There is a common misconception that traveling with pets, especially dogs, isn't possible. In reality, it is easy to bring Fido along for the ride! Van lifers who have active breeds find it easy to exercise and stimulate their dogs when they camp in national and state parks where there are endless hiking trails. And, if urban camping is more your style, then you will be able to find free dog parks in most major cities.

Of course, traveling with a pet will take up some extra space in the van, so you'll need to accommodate that when converting the van. Ensuring that your animal behaves appropriately while driving is another factor. Some animals only associate rides in the car with the vet or the kennel. If you need to un-train that behavior from your pet, then start taking drives to fun destinations—like the park or a coffee shop for a pup cup —or taking drives just for the sake of going around the block a few times. Give your pet enrichment treats while you drive to distract and calm them.

Solo van lifers especially appreciate the chance to bring their pets on this journey. Animals can offer companionship when you are camping alone, both rurally and in urban settings. Some people view their dogs as a source of protection, too. Dogs are sure to start barking and growling when they hear a disturbance outside the van.

Crate training your pet, if they aren't already, is an essential step to keeping them safe while on the road. Some van lifers find creative ways to build their pet's crates, especially dog crates, into the cabinetry and storage of the van. The first step is to determine the correct size of crate for your pet. They should be able to turn in a full circle comfortably within the crate. Make sure to include blankets or beds to make the crate feel cozy; whatever soft item you include will depend on your animal's personality. Some dogs chew or destroy blankets and beds, and ingesting the stuffing or fabric is dangerous for them.

The first few times you coax your animal into the crate, use treats as a motivator. When the crate door is closed, play crate games and slip food through the bars so they associate the crate with positive reinforcements. The crate should be a safe space that they can retreat to for rest and relaxation, as well as being a safe spot for you to keep them when you are out of the van.

Start with small steps. The first time you leave them alone in the crate only leave for a few minutes, then a bit longer, and longer. Going away for multiple hours of errands the first time they are in their crate will cause extra anxiety, but running out for a cup of coffee and coming right back is an appropriate amount of time for their first experience alone in the crate. Soon, you'll be able to leave them alone for long amounts of time. Just be patient with your pet!

There are a few extra considerations van lifers need to make when traveling with pets. For instance, double-check all park and campground rules prior to making your camping reservations. Not every campground, state, or national park will allow pets. Service animals are always an exception. Plan ample bathroom breaks as you drive, too. You may have a bathroom on board the van or the ability to wait for the gas station in 20 miles, but your dog will need those extra potty breaks. Most pet stores sell pads for indoor potty breaks, but in a space as small as the van, that will start to smell very quickly.

Adding a pet to your van life experience will change your schedule and limit your flexibility, simply because they cannot be left unattended in

How to Live the Van Life Dream

the van for very long. This could rule out certain hikes, adventures, or prolonged grocery shopping trips. However, these extra steps shouldn't scare you away from embarking on van life simply because you have a pet. It just makes your experience all the more unique.

Chapter 8
Van Maintenance

Vehicle repairs can sneak up on you. They can be costly and take you off the road for several days. Anyone who has owned a car knows that preventative maintenance is the best way to reduce costly repairs. Preventative maintenance includes oil changes, fluid flushes, and tire rotations. Most of these basic practices can be handled at Jiffy Lubes and other mechanic chains across the country.

Before you hit the road, be sure to have a mechanic look over the van. If possible, get a mechanic to look over the van before you purchase it. The last thing you need is to find excessive repairs after you've purchased the van. Most sellers, especially individual people, won't have a problem with a mechanic giving the vehicle a once-over. If the seller is resistant to this request, don't pursue the transaction. They know something is wrong with the vehicle that they don't want you to find.

We'll cover a few of the basic steps to keeping the van in good running order, but I recommend picking up a book dedicated to auto repair. Or, you should watch a series of online videos so you are prepared if the van does break down while you are on the road. All van lifers should know how to change a tire, change their own oil, and jump the battery. You will rack up more miles on the van than a standard car, since you're living in it and traveling all across the country. These extra miles will mean extra wear and tear on the van.

How to Live the Van Life Dream

To change a tire, you'll need a car jack, a spare tire, and a wrench. If you still have the vehicle's owner manual, that may help in your specific situation. Not all vans or tires are the same. Pull over to a safe location, put on your hazards and the parking brake, and gather your materials. If you invested in those hazard cones or flags we discussed in Chapter 6, it is a good time to put those to use.

First, you'll need to remove the hubcap or wheel cover if there is one. The lug nuts are behind this cover. It should pop off from the pressure of the flat end of your wrench. Refer to your owner's manual for vehicle-specific recommendations. Next, use your wrench to loosen the lug nuts. The lug nuts will probably be tightly secured, so don't be afraid to throw a lot of weight behind your wrench. They don't need to be removed fully at this point, just a half of a full turn. Once the lug nuts have been loosened, you can put the car jack in place and raise the car roughly six inches off the ground.

With that corner of the car lifted off the ground, you can finish unscrewing the lug nuts. They should unscrew easier now than before. To pull off the tire, grab it by the tread on either side. Pull towards yourself slowly and it should come away from the hub behind it. Once removed, place the tire face down on the ground so it doesn't roll away. You can line up the spare by keeping the rim in line with the holes for the lug nuts. Push it on until the lug nuts are able to be screwed back on. As soon as the spare has been secured by the lug nuts, lower the jack so the van's wheels return to the ground. Put the hubcap back on; it should still fit with the spare.

Before hitting the road again, check the air pressure in the spare tire. Make sure you head towards an auto shop so they can patch your tire if possible or install a new tire.

You'll need jumper cables to jump the van if the battery dies. You'll also need a second vehicle, which can make jumping the van's battery difficult when you are on the road or far from the next town. Once a friend comes to the rescue or a kind soul stops their driving to give you a hand, arrange the vehicles so the jumper cables can reach from one engine to the next. Make sure to safely judge the situation if someone pulls off on the side of the road to help. If you feel uncomfortable, call a service like AAA.

Take the keys out of both vehicles and open the hoods. Find the batteries, typically located amongst the engine, and the positive and negative ports on each battery. Connect the red jumper cable to the positive end of each battery and the black jumper cable to the negative end of only the charged car battery. The black jumper cable should be attached to a grounding force in the dead van battery. Some vehicles have a specific spot labeled for grounding; if the van does not have this, then attach the jumper cable to a standard, grounded piece of metal. The owner's manual should specify whether or not there is a dedicated grounding piece.

Once all the cables are in place, start the car with the charged battery. Allow it to run for a few minutes as the charge flows from one car to the other. After a few minutes, turn the key in the ignition of the van with the dead battery. It may take a few tries as the battery charges. Once the van is able to turn on and run for a few minutes, you can remove the jumper cables. Take the cables off the previously dead battery first. Start with the black jumper cable, then remove the red jumper cable. Repeat the same process for the battery from the charged vehicle. Store away the cables and contact a mechanic to see if you need to get the van looked at by a professional.

Changing the oil in the van is the basic maintenance chore that requires the most automotive skill. That doesn't mean an average van lifer can't learn how to change oil by themselves!

The specific steps for each model of van may be slightly different, so consult a professional before jumping into your first oil change. We'll cover the basic steps here. These should be similar across most makes and models of vans.

You need to purchase a few materials before starting the oil change process. An oil filter, an oil catch pan, and a new container of oil are essential for completing an oil change safely. The professionals at an AutoZone or similar automotive store should be able to help you pick out the appropriate filter and pan for your van. Unlike the jumper cables or car jack for our previous two tasks, these items are not reusable, so you'll need to purchase new ones every time you change the oil in the van.

Once you have all of your materials, turn off the van, lift the van on a jack, open the hood, and locate the dipstick. A dipstick measures the amount of usable oil left in the van. It will need to be removed for this process. Next, take the oil pan and lower yourself under the van. You need to locate the engine oil pan that should be underneath the car. On the side of that pan will be a drain plug; some cars and vans have two drain plugs. Loosen the plug with a wrench to allow the used oil to flow out of the pan. Position the oil catch pan right below the drain plug so the oil won't splash everywhere. It may take a few minutes for all of the oil to drain out of the van. When all of the oil has drained, replace the drain plug. Screw it on tightly!

Next, find the oil filter. This will likely be underneath the car, just like the engine oil pan. Loosen the oil filter and allow any oil within the filter to drain into your oil catch pan. Once fully removed, make sure you've also removed the filter gasket.

Apply a thin layer of new oil to the gasket before replacing it along with the new filter. Turn clockwise to tighten and secure in place.

Back on top of the car, open the oil container cap located in the engine. Pour your new oil into the container. Screw the cap back onto the container, replace the dipstick, and start the van. Allow it to run for a few minutes to ensure all of the oil is flowing properly. Check for leaks, and if you find any, immediately shut off the vehicle to inspect. If you don't see any active leaks, turn off the engine and continue to check for leaks once the oil settles.

The easiest way to dispose of old oil is to drop it off at the nearest Jiffy Lube, Walmart, or other oil change center. They will have the proper methods for disposal. Never dispose of oil down a drain or leave it in nature as oil is destructive to natural environments. How often you need to change your oil will depend on the miles you are driving and the quality of oil you are putting in the van.

Tools and Essentials You Need to Stay Moving

Knowing how to complete basic repairs on the van yourself is great, but without the right tools to get the job done, you will still be stranded. You should keep a toolbox in the van to make simple repairs both inside and outside. When assembling the toolbox, consider the space you have available. Some items are non-negotiable, but others are rentable from auto repair stores.

Jumper Cables

These belong in the essential category. Without jumper cables, you cannot jump the van's battery, and it is risky to assume that whoever comes to your rescue will have the proper cables. You can purchase jumper cables from any brick-and-mortar auto store or Amazon.

Consider length when purchasing these. Of course, longer cables will require extra space for storage, but they will come in handy when and if your battery dies. Most cables are available in 12-foot and 20-foot versions.

Wrenches, Screwdrivers, and Other Small Tools

Smaller tools like wrenches, screwdrivers, hammers, and pliers are useful for engine repairs, flat tires, and oil changes. But, they can also come in handy inside the van. If your bed frame breaks, a drawer comes loose, or some other built-in storage compartment needs repair, you'll be relying on handheld tools like these to get the job done.

Keep screws and nails around as well. A screwdriver without screws or a hammer without nails won't be much help when something breaks.

Bungee Cords and Other Securing Devices

You have a lot of items stored in the van, and you may acquire more along the way. Bungee cords, tape, and 'S' hooks can keep your items in place when you are storing extra stuff in the van or if you need to secure boxes on top of the van. They can also come in handy if you find yourself the unhappy victim of an accident and need to secure a door, bumper, or side mirror.

Hazard Cones and Safety Equipment

If you break down at night before you've made it to camp, then you'll want reflective cones or flags to set on the van. You may also want a reflective vest for yourself so other drivers can see you if you are changing a flat tire after sundown or before sunrise.

Safety equipment like this can be purchased from brick-and-mortar auto stores and online from Amazon. They may seem excessive, but safety is very important, especially if you need to make a van repair far from well-lit roads or the nearest towns. Vests and flags should not take up much storage space, so they are well worth the money.

Conclusion

At the end of the road, when the key is out of the ignition and the sun is setting on the Western horizon, you will have put the van in park with all of the best knowledge at your disposal.

That night, whether you are camped in the beauties of nature or camped in the utility of a parking lot, you will be able to cook dinner, clean up, and unwind, all from the comfort of your van.

Now you know the answers to everyone's most pressing questions: "Where do you sleep?" "How do you go to the bathroom?" and "How can you live in that small space?" Together we covered the basics of converting a van, from plumbing to electrical, and how to buy a pre-built model. We dove into the budget of a van lifer and some basic passive income tips that can transform any van life journey. We took van life to the technology age with internet options and the most-used apps for making the most of life on the road. From there, you got a crash course in van maintenance and the skills everyone needs to be safe on the road. Embracing van life is a big decision, but it doesn't have to be a scary one. I hope at the end of this book, you can begin your dream of living in a van with confidence.

It has been a long journey, but maybe not as long as your next van life road trip. There is a whole world to see: beautiful countryside, powerful mountains, and salty seas. None of it will come to you from your well-

Conclusion

worn seat on the couch and your office job. So, if you are considering leaving it all behind to pursue the van life of your dreams, embrace wanderlust, and see the world before it passes you by, I hope that my advice and tips have helped sway you in the right direction.

If you've just embarked on this journey, then remember the following checklist:

- Find the van that is right for you, whether it is pre-built or in need of a conversion.
- Convert and update your van with the proper tools for installing electrical wiring, pipes, and insulation.
- Stay connected with the best internet and data options on the road.
- Be on budget every month with passive income.
- Keep the van in good running order by learning how to deal with basic repairs.

If you have been converting a van or planning your trip for a while, then you can implement the advice from this book at any point in your van life journey.

Road Trips and Destinations

As a final recommendation, I'd like to suggest a few roads-less-traveled that may inspire the routes and destinations you explore while living in the van. Some of these trips include the 'must-see' spots in America, others are off the beaten path, but all will be sure to leave you speechless.

Route 66

Route 66 is one of the most famous roads in the world. It is more than 2,400 miles long, and it guides travelers through eight states including Illinois, Missouri, New Mexico, Arizona, and California. The road begins in Chicago, Illinois and it ends in Santa Monica, California.

Conclusion

You can speedily explore Route 66 as fast as you can, or spend two or more weeks cruising down the Mother Road. This historic tour stops through many can't miss roadside attractions and cities. After starting in Chicago, you can explore St. Louis, Missouri, Oklahoma City, Oklahoma, and San Bernardino, California. In between these fun-filled cities, travelers can see Cadillac Ranch, the world's largest ketchup bottle, and the National Cowboy Museum.

If you choose to embark on this adventure, it will be filled with mostly urban camping, but there will be some campsites along the way, especially the further west you travel. It may not have the same great views as some other destinations, but traveling down Route 66 will make you feel like you've joined a part of history.

Florida Keys Highway 1

Unlike the incredibly lengthy drive down Route 66, driving Highway 1 from Miami to Key West only takes three hours. The highway is 113 miles long and will take you to the southernmost point of the continental United States.

This salt-air Sunday drive includes 42 bridges that connect 34 Keys, including the Seven Mile Bridge at Marathon Key.

There are tons of attractions to see on every Key, so if you want to stretch out your Florida Keys road trip, you can use several days to get to Key West. There is the Caribbean Club and the Coral Reef State Park in Key Largo, the Dolphin Research Center in Marathon Key, and dozens of beaches on every island. If you are looking to sneak in a night of rural camping, be sure to stop at Bahia Honda Key. They allow camping in Bahia Honda State Park. There's nothing like waking up next to crashing waves.

Obviously, the final destination for Highway 1 is Key West, the southernmost point in the United States. Key West offers beautiful beaches, historic downtown boulevards, and fun activities like parasailing. They also have some of the best key lime pie in the world.

Conclusion

The traffic on this highway can get intense on the weekends, so try to plan your drive for a weekday. If you can't avoid a weekend trip, then be sure to leave early in the morning so you can cruise without worrying about bumper-to-bumper traffic ruining your peaceful ocean drive.

The Oregon Coast

Now shifting our attention from the east coast to the west coast, van lifers shouldn't skip the picturesque views on the Oregon coastline. Historic Highway 101 follows Oregon's coastline north and south. Even if you never get out of the van, this drive is beautiful. The coast can be split into three sections, you can travel the whole route, or you can split it into smaller trips, whatever works for you.

The southern section of Oregon's coast begins at the California-Oregon border and ends at Reedsport. The central stretch of the coast lies between Reedsport to Cascade Head. Finally, the northern stretch lies from Cascade Head to the Columbia River. The full road trip is just over 300 miles. Once again, this is achievable in a day if you don't stop and look around.

The key sites to see along the way include Ecola State Park, where you can embark on scenic heights and roam the oceanside hills all day long. From there, grab a bite to eat from the Tillamook Creamery. Tillamook, Oregon is famous for its ice creams and cheeses. After you've stuffed yourself with dairy, stop at Cape Kiwanda for gorgeous views and massive crashing waves. Check the Sea Lion Caves off your list, too. Near Heceta Head Lighthouse, visitors can descend into the Sea Lion Caves, some of the largest sea caves in the country, and spot the sea lions that call the area home.

There is no shortage of beauty and brilliant natural sites along the coast of Oregon. It is an ideal trip for those who want to camp rurally but stay near civilization too.

Conclusion

New England's Fall Colors Drive

If you are headed back east, make sure to check out New England while the leaves are changing colors. The region of New England includes Connecticut, Massachusetts, Maine, Rhode Island, Vermont, and New Hampshire. For the best fall colors, I recommend Vermont, Maine, and New Hampshire, specifically. As an added tip, stay clear of the major cities; you'll find the best colors out in the hills and countryside of these states.

The Kancamagus Highway in New Hampshire is a great mini-road trip to start your larger fall colors adventure. New Hampshire in general has great hiking trails tucked among its mountain ranges. There will be no shortage of beautiful camping areas here.

Once you've made your way up to Maine, Acadia National Park will also have beautiful colors, excellent hiking, and easy to access camping. Making the time for Maine on this trip in general is important, because it is the most remote of all the New England states and it isn't easy to get to.

Other key stops in your New England road trip can include Stowe, Vermont, Manchester, Vermont, and Lake Winnipesaukee, New Hampshire.

Time your New England trip so that you can see the colors at their 'peak.' Typically the peak is the first week of October, but do your research before you head that way because every year is a bit different. Thankfully for van lifers, you won't need to worry about up-priced and crowded hotels: You're traveling with your home! The fall is a popular time to visit New England specifically for the beautiful foliage, so this trip won't necessarily be one that finds you peace and quiet. Hopefully, the visual beauty makes up for it.

Upper Peninsula of Michigan

The Upper Peninsula of Michigan, otherwise known as the UP, is home to gorgeous forests, a picturesque lakefront, and quaint little towns. I

Conclusion

can't believe more people don't give this road trip a shot. You'll start in Mackinac Island, Michigan and end in St. Ignace, Michigan. It makes a nearly perfect circle throughout the UP.

Mackinac Island is one of the more touristy spots on this road trip, but the car-free, quaint island is a must-see. You can dress up and dine at the Inn, take a carriage ride, and head to Mystery Spot for some zipline-style adventure. When you are ready to leave Mackinac Island you will take a scenic drive over a five mile long bridge to the remainder of the UP.

From there, head to Sault Ste. Marie. This town borders Canada—seriously, half the town is in Michigan and the other half is in Canada. If you are feeling adventurous and want to cross the border, go for it! They have a river museum, historic locks, and ample camping parks.

On the other side of the UP, you'll find a hike to Mount Arvon, the highest point in all of Michigan. If you would rather find a scenic drive than an active hike, try the 10-mile Brockway Mountain Drive.

No matter what other towns you visit along the Lakeshore Drive, the road that outlines most of the UP, make sure to taste the local fare: seafood. And, count as many lighthouses as possible!

Tour of South Texas

Howdy partner! If you want to check out the Lone Star State, but avoid the typical sites and touristy crowds, then this is the road trip for you. Located as far south as you can get in Texas, right along the Rio Grande River Valley and the Texas-Mexico border, you will find six fun, outdoorsy, and memorable stops that you can't see anywhere else in the world.

Begin your trip in the Bentsen Rio Grande State Park. It stretches for miles along the Texas-Mexico border. Not far from the state park is the National Butterfly Center. Visitors can spot dozens of different butterflies, and all of these butterflies attract some tropical bird species to the area as well. As you continue driving, you'll reach Boca Chica State Park. This state park has miles and miles of beaches and a wildlife refuge island.

Conclusion

The journey will continue to lead you to sand and surf as you head to Sao Paulo Island and the nation's largest sandcastle. From Sao Paulo, drive north to Laguna Atascosa Wildlife Preserve. Hiking and fishing enthusiasts will thrive in this preserve. They allow camping too!

Of course, to reach this short and sweet road trip in the south of Texas, you'll find yourself driving through the rest of this massive state. Make stops in the popular cities of Austin and San Antonio to see the capital and the Alamo. If you want to experience nature in the Texas Hill Country, then Enchanted Rock State Park offers beautiful views and moderately taxing hikes.

Beartooth Scenic Highway, Montana

If you are looking to explore the Rocky Mountains, then look no further than Beartooth Scenic Highway. This highway pass loops through the ridges of the Rockies, reaching more than 10,000 feet in elevation.

The road starts in Montana and ends in Wyoming near an entrance to Yellowstone National Park, so if you are looking to cross Yellowstone off your bucket list, this road trip could be the perfect way to get there.

Cycling, skiing, and snowmobiling are incredibly popular activities along this highway full of switchbacks and curves. Drive carefully! There are also dozens of hiking trails accessible from the side of the road that allow you to take an even closer look at the beautiful nature of Montana and Wyoming. The Beartooth Scenic Highway is the shortest trip on our list, but it is one of the most beautiful ones.

Cooke City, one of the towns located along the route, holds fun festivals throughout the year. They have several campgrounds and trailheads, too. Throughout the year visitors can experience the Festival of Nations, which celebrates immigrants and their national heritages, the Spring Fling, and the Mountain Man Rendezvous. Mountain Man harkens back to the olden days of fur trapping and trading from the 19th century and earlier. Both of these eclectic festivals offer unique foods and other once-in-a-lifetime experiences.

Conclusion

I hope you enjoy these road trip options and return to the chapters you need most to prepare for the trip again and again. Continue referencing this helpful guide once you are on the road, too. You never know when you'll need a refresher on changing a tire or preparing your morning coffee. And, if any of the specific sections on passive income caught your eye, be sure to check out my other book, *The Ultimate Van Life Guide to Passive Income*. With my help, you can not only master the van life dream, but you can earn a living the passive way.

Happy trails!

Thank you for taking the time to read this book. If you found value in the pages you've just read, it would be greatly appreciated if you could leave a review on Amazon.

If you would like to work with me or if you have any questions, feel free to reach out to me at my email jake@coffeyandrader.com

Sign Up Bonus

Just scan the QR code to be the first to know when I launch another book on travel, real estate, or passive income!

As a special bonus, you'll receive:

Top 10 Passive Income Ideas for Building Wealth in 2023
13 Essentials You Need To Know About Before Buying Your First RV

absolutely FREE!

Bibliography

7 of the best budgeting tips. (n.d.). NerdWallet. Retrieved May 23, 2022, from https://www.nerdwallet.com/article/finance/budgeting-tips

11 most important tools for a diy van conversion—The wanderful. (n.d.). Retrieved May 23, 2022, from https://thewanderful.co/blog/11-most-important-tools-you-need-for-a-diy-van-conversion

A legendary Oregon coast road trip: 35 stops & 3 itineraries! (2019, October 29). Oregon Is for Adventure. https://oregonisforadventure.com/oregon-coast-road-trip/

Bor, K. (2020, April 5). Best vans for van life: Sprinter vs transit vs promaster. *Bearfoot Theory*. https://bearfoottheory.com/best-vans-for-van-life/

Bor, K. (2021, April 25). Van life cooking: How to meal plan & cook in a small space. *Bearfoot Theory*. https://bearfoottheory.com/van-life-cooking/

Custom build van process. (n.d.). Custom Van Builder | Vanlife Customs. Retrieved May 23, 2022, from https://vanlifecustoms.com/custombuild

Diy van insulation for a campervan conversion | how to install insulation. (2018, October 27). https://www.parkedinparadise.com/insulate-van/

Driving directions, traffic reports & carpool rideshares by waze. (n.d.). Retrieved May 23, 2022, from https://www.waze.com/company/

Gym memberships | austin (S i-hwy 35), tx | planet fitness. (n.d.). Retrieved May 23, 2022, from https://www.planetfitness.com/gyms/austin-s-i-hwy-35-tx/offers

How to budget for vanlife | van conversion & monthly budget. (2020, April 29). *Two Roaming Souls*. https://tworoamingsouls.com/how-to-budget-for-vanlife-van-conversion-monthly-budget/

How to build your van water & plumbing systems. (2020, May 9). *Chasing the Wild Goose*. https://www.chasingthewildgoose.com/van-water-plumbing/

How to change a flat tire. (n.d.). Retrieved May 23, 2022, from https://www.bridgestonetire.com/learn/maintenance/how-to-change-a-flat-tire/

How to change your oil. (n.d.). Retrieved May 23, 2022, from https://www.pennzoil.com/en_us/education/know-your-oil/changing-your-own-oil.html

http://1140055779375581. (2021, December 13). *Epic guide to van life electrical & solar(For diy campervans)*. https://gnomadhome.com/van-build-solar-electrical-wiring/

Lawrence, K. (2021, March 4). *The ultimate texas hidden gem road trip will take you to 6 incredible little-known spots in the state*. OnlyInYourState. https://www.onlyinyourstate.com/texas/hidden-gem-road-trip-tx/

Nov 05, S. S., Nov 05, 2021 | 3 Minutes, &. Minutes, 2021 | 3. (n.d.). *How to crate train your dog in nine easy steps*. American Kennel Club. Retrieved May 23, 2022, from https://www.akc.org/expert-advice/training/how-to-crate-train-your-dog-in-9-easy-steps/

One of the best american road trips is hiding out in michigan. (n.d.). Thrillist. Retrieved May 23, 2022, from https://www.thrillist.com/travel/nation/michigan-upper-peninsula-road-trip

Bibliography

Passive income. (n.d.). Investopedia. Retrieved May 23, 2022, from https://www.investopedia.com/terms/p/passiveincome.asp

Petersen |, J. (2021, April 28). *Vanlife safety and security: Personal, property and preparation | vansage*. VanSage.Com: Campervan Gear, Vanlife Wisdom. https://vansage.com/vanlife-safety-and-security/

Pietsch, B. (2021, April 2). How veterans of #vanlife feel about all the newbies. *The New York Times*. https://www.nytimes.com/2021/04/02/us/living-in-a-van-coronavirus-pandemic.html

Portable power station for your campervan. (2018, August 31). *Weekender Van Life*. https://weekendervanlife.com/portable-power-stations-for-van-life/

Road tripping Montana's beartooth scenic highway. (n.d.). Matador Network. Retrieved May 23, 2022, from https://matadornetwork.com/trips/roadtripping-montana-the-beartooth-scenic-highway/

Sprinter model vans. (n.d.). Mercedes-Benz Vans. Retrieved May 23, 2022, from https://www.mbvans.com/en/sprinter

Swartzlander, D. (2021, May 25). *Best stops on a Florida Keys road trip itinerary*. The Planet D: Adventure Travel Blog. https://theplanetd.com/florida-keys-road-trip-itinerary/

The top 14 vanlife apps for the ultimate road trip. (2019, September 30). *Chasing the Wild Goose*. https://www.chasingthewildgoose.com/vanlife-apps/

The ultimate guide to route 66. (n.d.). Roadtrippers. Retrieved May 23, 2022, from https://roadtrippers.com/the-ultimate-guide-route-66/

The wanderful. (n.d.). Retrieved May 23, 2022, from https://thewanderful.co/blog/sprinter-van-bathroom-options

Upgrade to pro | alltrails. (n.d.). AllTrails.Com. Retrieved May 23, 2022, from https://www.alltrails.com/pro

Van life lessons in minimalism. (n.d.). Without Waste Shop. Retrieved May 23, 2022, from https://withoutwasteshop.com/blogs/news/lessons-in-minimalism-from-living-in-a-van

Vanlife laundry: A laundry list of clothes cleaning hacks. (n.d.). Always the Adventure. Retrieved May 23, 2022, from https://alwaystheadventure.com/vanlife/van-laundry

Vanlife with dogs, cats & other pets—Things to know before you go. (2020, December 11). *Backpacking Like A Boss*. https://www.backpackinglikeaboss.com/vanlife-with-pets-dogs-cats/

Why we set intentions in yoga and meditation practice. (n.d.). Verywell Mind. Retrieved May 23, 2022, from https://www.verywellmind.com/why-we-set-intentions-in-yoga-and-meditation-practice-5205511

Printed in Great Britain
by Amazon